Paranormal Field

HOW TO FIND GHOSTS

Thomas Kingsley Troupe

Hi Jinx is published by Black Rabbit Books
P.O. Box 227, Mankato, Minnesota, 56002.
www.blackrabbitbooks.com

Marysa Storm, editor; Michael Sellner, designer
and photo researcher

Library of Congress Cataloging-in-Publication Data
Names: Troupe, Thomas Kingsley, author.
Title: How to find ghosts / by Thomas Kingsley Troupe.
Description: Mankato, Minnesota : Black Rabbit Books, [2023] |
Series: Hi jinx. Paranormal field guides | Includes bibliographical references
and index. | Audience: Ages: 8-12 | Audience: Grades: 4-6 |
Summary: "With fun facts, a colorful design, and critical thinking questions,
How to Find Ghosts inspires readers to take their love of the paranormal to
the next level all while laughing and learning"- Provided by publisher.
Identifiers: LCCN 2020034522 (print) | LCCN 2020034523 (ebook) |
ISBN 9781623107185 (hardcover) | ISBN 9781644665671 (paperback) |
ISBN 9781623107246 (ebook)
Subjects: LCSH: Ghosts–Juvenile literature. | Parapsychology–Juvenile
literature | Parapsychology. sears
Classification: LCC BF1461 .T763 2022 (print) | LCC BF1461 (ebook) |
DDC 133.1-dc23
LC record available at https://lccn.loc.gov/2020034522
LC ebook record available at https://lccn.loc.gov/2020034523

Image Credits

Alamy: Alexander Caminada, 10; Shutterstock: Aleksandr Bryliaev, 4, 14, 18; AlexanderTrou, 12, 13; Arcady, 12, 16; benchart, 6–7; Christos Georghiou, Cover; Dualororua, Cover, 6–7; ekler, 11; freesoulproduction, 12–13; Galyna G, 3, 4, 7, 12, 13, 18, 19; HitToon, Cover, 1; Hollygraphic, 14; klyaksun, 8–9; Liusa, 20; Memo Angeles, 5, 6, 7, 17, 19; monbibi, 4, 5, 14, 18; Multipedia, 17; My Life Graphic, 5, 10, 18–19; Nearbirds, Cover; Ori Artiste, 1, 5, 21; Pasko Maksim, 23, 24; Pitju, 9, 17, 21; Ron Dale, 3, 4, 8, 15, 20; schwarzhana, 2, 3, 14, 23; tani85fr, 5, 21; Tartila, Cover, 6, 7; totallypic, 5, 17; vectorpouch, 18–19

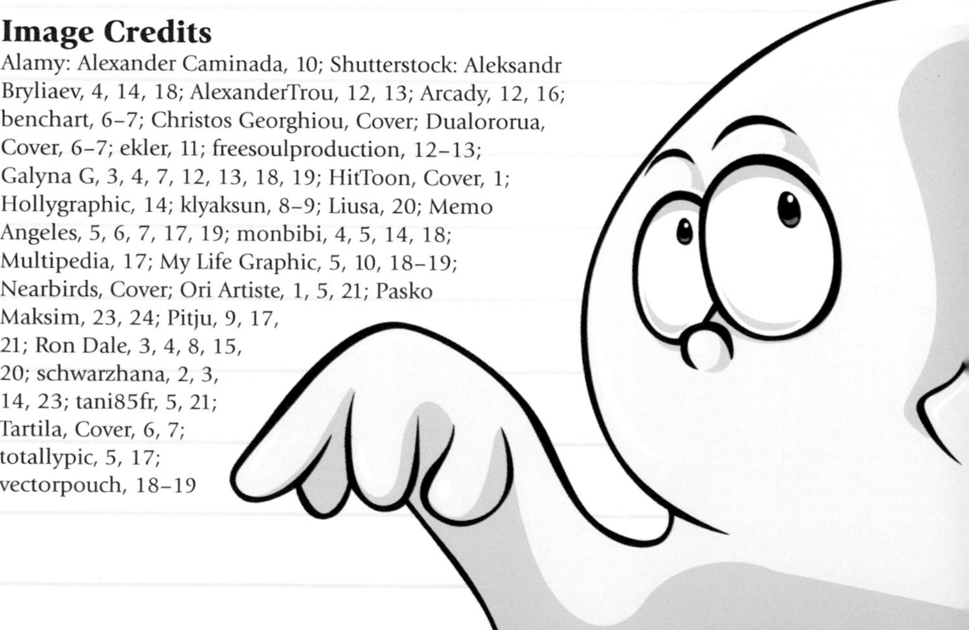

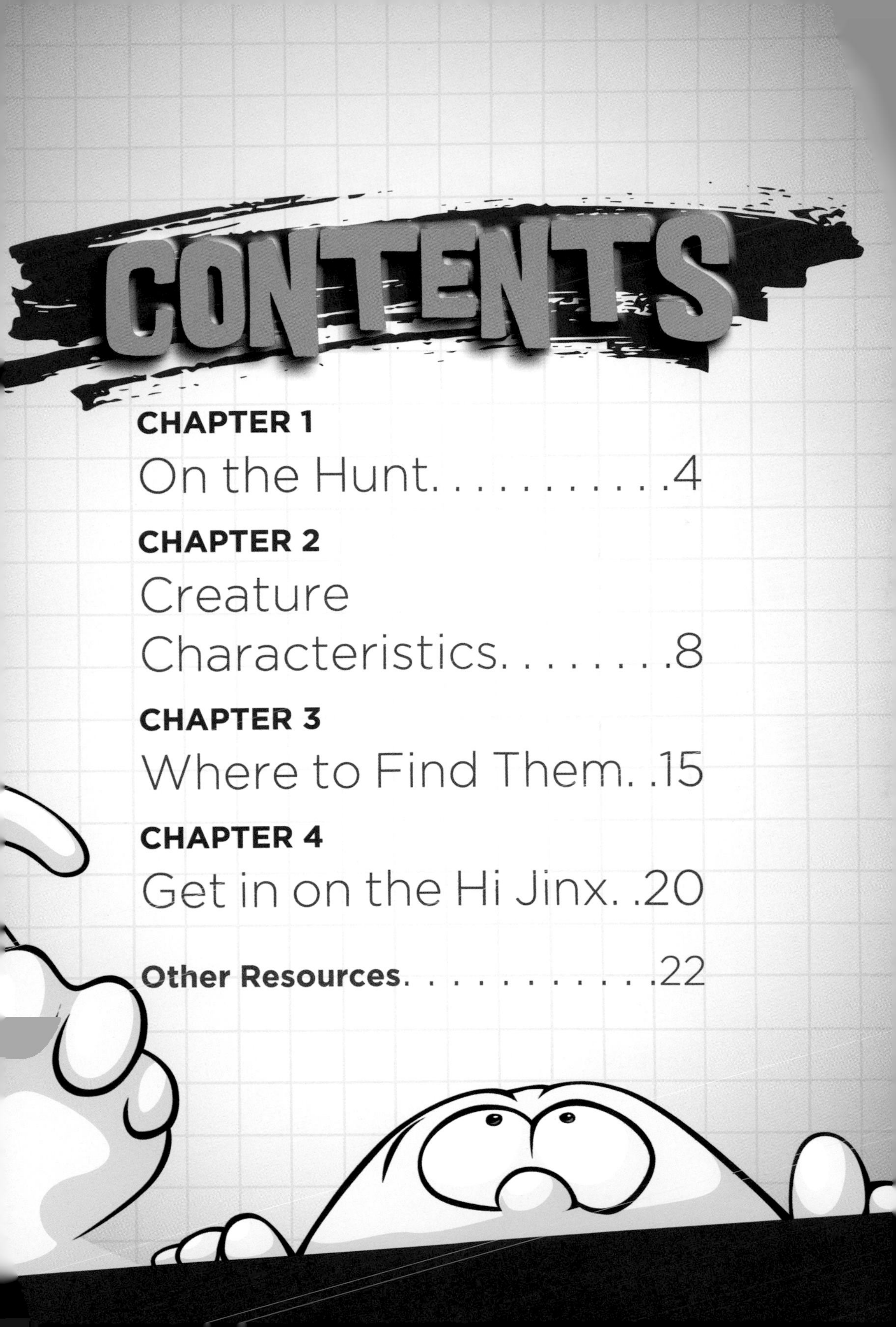

CONTENTS

Chapter 1

ON THE HUNT

Well, if it isn't the future world's second-best ghost hunter. You know, since I'm number one. I'm glad you're hunting for some hauntings. Many people don't even believe in ghosts. I am not one of those people. I've seen hundreds of ghosts!* If you want to find some **phantoms**, you've picked up the right book. My field guide is your key to spooky searching.

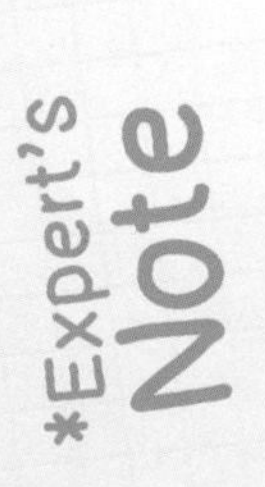

I lost count sometime after 739.

Meet the Expert

Thomas Kingsley Troupe

Thomas Kingsley Troupe **claims** to be an expert ghost hunter. According to him, he's experienced all sorts of **paranormal** activity. He even said he *had* tons of **evidence**. But then it disappeared. He's certain ghosts must have taken it. We're not so sure.

Handy and Helpful

Okay, let's slow down for a second. I know you're new to this ghost hunting thing. But I'm telling you, my guide can help you. We're going to cover everything **eerie** about ghosts. You'll learn what to look for and what to do.

So keep this book handy on your adventures. It's like having me right beside you, holding the flashlight. And I promise I won't yell "BOO" just to scare you!

Chapter 2

CREATURE CHARACTERISTICS

To hunt ghosts, you need to know what you're looking for. That's tough, though. Ghosts take many different forms. Some look like faded people or bursts of light. Others are completely invisible. Basically, if something looks or feels weird, it could be a ghost. But if your cookies go missing, don't blame ghosts. There's probably a simple explanation. Maybe your dad ate them.

Behaviors

Not all ghosts behave the same way. Some of them make noises. Others move objects. Some experts think ghosts do these things to **communicate** with us. They might have a message for the living. If you're quiet enough, ghostly voices can be recorded.

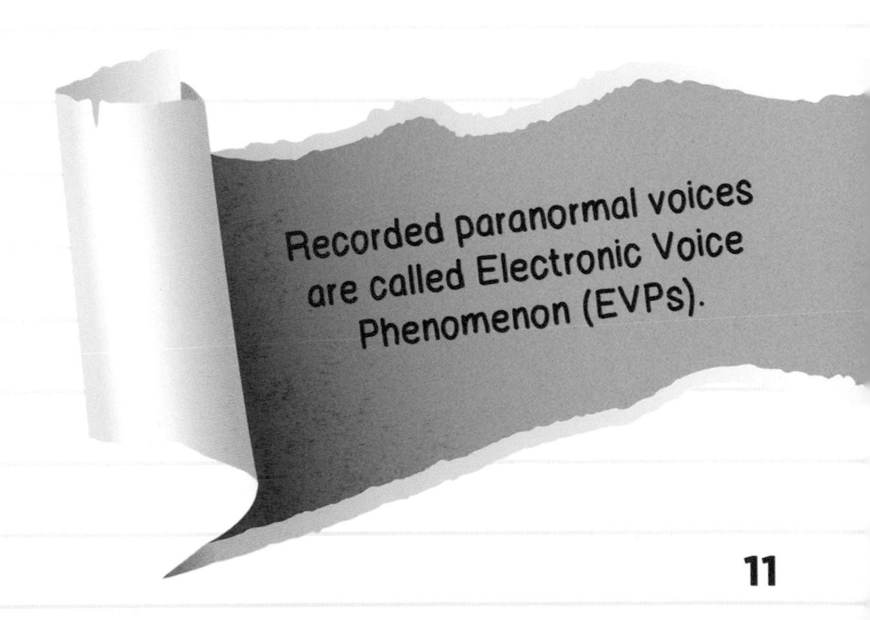

Diet

When you're dead, you're not hungry anymore. You know, unless you're a zombie.* That means ghosts don't really need to eat. They do seem to feed off energy, though. I often **detect** ghosts near radio and TV waves. Try **luring** ghosts using old TVs and radios.

*Expert's Note

Stay tuned! I'm working on a guide about finding zombies next.

*Expert's Note
If you are afraid, just bring a stuffed animal with you. I always bring my trusty stuffed elephant, Bubba, when I go ghost hunting.

Chapter 3

WHERE TO FIND THEM

I don't mean to scare you, but ghosts could be anywhere. They don't just hang around haunted houses or graveyards. A ghost might be a homeowner who isn't ready to leave. Sometimes they appear in places where bad things happened, like prisons.

Don't be afraid, readers!* I'm not saying EVERY place is haunted. Most ghosts just tend to stay where they died. Others stay near places they visited a lot when they were alive.

Tracking Ghosts

Ghost hunting is easiest at night. Things are quieter when the world is asleep. You'll have a better chance at hearing ghosts whisper. You can also track ghosts with one simple tool. A thermometer. Check for cold spots. Colder temperatures can mean a ghost is nearby.*

***Expert's Note**

Once, I thought a ghost haunted my basement. Turns out I just left the freezer door open.

thermometer

Approaching Ghosts

When approaching ghosts, keep quiet! Ghosts have faint voices. Be respectful too. Don't treat ghosts like monsters. Remember ghosts were people once too! It's not a bad idea to ask before taking photos. I didn't, and now a ghost named Margie haunts my bathroom.*

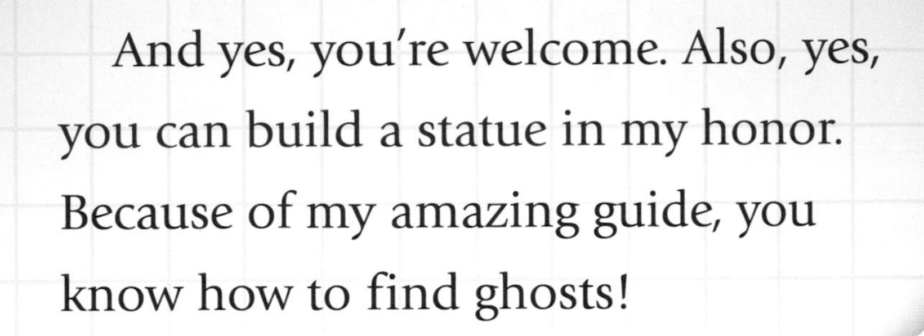

And yes, you're welcome. Also, yes, you can build a statue in my honor. Because of my amazing guide, you know how to find ghosts!

Chapter 4

GET IN ON THE HI JINX

No one has been able to prove ghosts are real. But don't give up the hunt! Get permission to explore old places. Visit your library to read books about hauntings. Watch videos from other ghost hunters. Maybe you'll uncover the truth!

Take It One Step More

1. Do you believe in ghosts? Why or why not?

2. If you could talk to the ghost of anyone who's died, who would you pick? Why?

3. Some people think ghosts can't leave certain spots. Why do you think that is?

GLOSSARY

claim (KLAYM)—to say something is true when some people might say it's not true

communicate (kuh-MYU-nuh-kayt)—to share information, thoughts, or feelings so they are understood

detect (dee-TEKT)—to discover the existence or presence of something

eerie (EER-ee)—strange and mysterious

evidence (EH-vuh-dens)—something that proves something else exists or is true

lure (LUHR)—to attract someone or something to an area

paranormal (par-uh-NAWR-muhl)—very strange and not able to be explained by what scientists know about nature and the world

phantom (FAN-tuhm)—something that appears to be real but has no physical existence